AF103428

This Notebook Belongs To

____

Copyright © 2019 RWG

All rights reserved.

www.ingramcontent.com/pod-product-compliance
Lightning Source LLC
LaVergne TN
LVHW061940070526
838199LV00060B/3900
* 9 7 8 9 5 8 3 1 3 4 5 5 5 *